My First Words
A - Z
English to Spanish

Bilingual Learning Made Fun and Easy with Words and Pictures

by Sharon Purtill

Books

 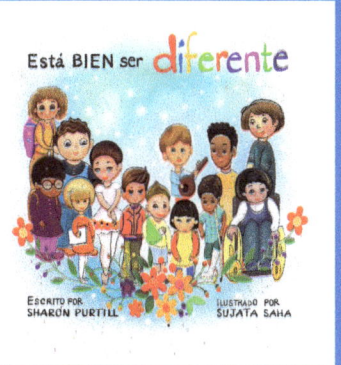

libros

mis primeras palabras
inglés a español

My First Words A-Z
English to Spanish

Bilingual Learning Made Fun and
Easy with Words and Pictures

by Sharon Purtill

Published by Dunhill Clare Publishing - Ontario, Canada
Copyright 2021 Dunhill Clare Publishing
dunhillclare@gmail.com

Edited by Marianna Horrisberger

All rights reserved. No part of this publication may be reproduced, stored in a retrieval system or transmitted, in any form or by any means, electronic, mechanical, photocopying, recording or otherwise without the prior permission of the copyright holder except when embodied in a brief review or mention.

Paperback edition   ISBN: 978-1-989733-74-5
Digital edition   ISBN: 978-1-989733-75-2

Library and Archives Canada Cataloguing in Publications

Apple

manzana

Books

libros

Cat

gato

Dog

perro

Elephant

elefante

Flower

flor

Hat

sombrero

Ice Cream

helado

Jacket

chaqueta/campera

Keys

llaves

Leaf

hoja

Milk

leche

Nest

nido

Orange

naranja

Pail

balde

Quilt

edredón

Rabbit

conejo

Shoe

zapato
zapatilla/tenis

Table

mesa

Umbrella

paraguas

Vacuum

aspiradora

Watermelon

sandía

Xylophone

xilófono

Yellow

amarillo

Zebra

cebra

Bonus Words

English and Spanish

Let's learn common words for things found in and around the home.

oh what
FUN

Found in the Kitchen
que se encuentra en la cocina

plate	plato
fork	tenedor
spoon	cuchara
knife	cuchillo
bowl	bowl/tazón
cup	vaso

Found in the Bathroom
que se encuentra en el baño

toothpaste		pasta dental
toothbrush		cepillo de dientes
brush		cepillo
comb		peine
towel		toalla

Found in the Bedroom
que se encuentre en el dormitorio

bed	cama
blankets	mantas
pillow	almohada
dresser	vestidor
toys	juguetes

Found in the Living Room
encontrado en la sala de estar

television	televisión
chair	sillón
rug	alfombra
lamp	lámpara
sofa	sofá

Found Outside
encontrado afuera

tree		árbol
car		carro/auto
truck		camión
bike		bicicleta
grass		césped

www.ingramcontent.com/pod-product-compliance
Lightning Source LLC
Chambersburg PA
CBHW061203070526
44579CB00009B/112